Introspective

Michael Leunig was born in East Melbourne in 1945. He grew up near Footscray in Melbourne's industrial western suburbs.

Early influences include the ten volumes of Arthur Mee's children's encyclopedia; his dog, Dinah; the Maribyrnong River; and to some extent, Queen Elizabeth II who he saw passing by in Moonee Ponds in 1954 'looking very pale'.

The first book he read was *Shadow the Sheep Dog* by Enid Blyton.

Michael Leunig began working for newspapers in 1969 and has since published seven books. He lives in Melbourne.

Introspective

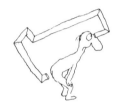

Michael Leunig

With a Foreword
by Helen Garner

Photographs of Michael Leunig
and his studio by Helga Salwe

The Text Publishing Company Pty Ltd
220 Clarendon Street
East Melbourne Victoria 3002
Australia

First published 1991

Designed by World of Wonders
Photography of drawings and paintings by Terence Bogue
Printed and bound at Griffin Press

National Library of Australia
Cataloguing-in-Publication data:
Leunig, Michael, 1945- .
Introspective.

ISBN 1 86372 200 9.

1. Leunig, Michael, 1945- - Exhibitions. 2.
Cartoonists - Australia - Exhibitions. 3. Caricatures
and cartoons - Australia - Exhibitions. I. Title.
741.5994

Introspective is published to accompany the exhibition 'A Michael Leunig Introspective'
presented by the 1991 Melbourne International Comedy Festival at the
National Gallery of Victoria.

The publisher acknowledges with gratitude the assistance of Jennifer Saunders,
exhibition co-ordinator at the Comedy Festival.

For there is a boundary to looking.
And the world that is looked at so deeply
wants to flourish in love.

Work of the eyes is done, now
go and do heart-work
on all the images imprisoned within you; for you
overpowered them: but even now you don't know them.
Learn, inner man, to look on your inner woman,
the one attained from a thousand
natures, the merely attained but
not yet beloved form.

Rainer Maria Rilke, 'Turning-point'

C o n t e n t s

F o r e w o r d

MICHAEL LEUNIG has been part of Melbourne's thoughts about itself for nearly twenty years. Since the seventies his drawings, clipped from newspapers and magazines, have outlasted everything else that we stuck to our kitchen notice-boards and fridge doors. Long after the paper they were printed on had stiffened and turned yellow, the pictures could snag attention and stir emotion at the most mundane moment of domestic life. Our children grew up knowing his work: it insinuated itself into our daily life here, it entered the vernacular and changed the way we thought about the world. We thought of him proudly as ours, in a special, intimate way.

But any smug civic ownership in which we might think to contain Leunig is smartly dissipated by the works collected here. He digs much deeper and flies much higher than my sentimental memories had given him credit for: in fact, I wonder now if I ever knew him at all.

Clearly Leunig has been a prisoner all this time, even in his books, of inadequate reproduction. The backs and margins of the original artwork are festooned with his pleas to technicians: 'strong contrast *please*; a sensative [sic] bromide please if possible', and to see his originals is to realise how *physical* his work is, its immediacy: the sharp delicacy of his grasses and flowers, the ethereal whiteness of his clouds, the dense layering of his dark and boiling skies.

But what impresses me even more, seeing the material here, is the depth of the archetypal structures it rests on and has always derived from; for now we see that Leunig from the beginning has persisted, consciously or otherwise, and perhaps against the pressure that all newspaper cartoonists must feel to be 'topical' or 'relevant', in using and re-using the imagery of the soul and the spirit. And why should the cartoon not be a natural form for this? 'Black,' wrote Odilon Redon, another struggler with the dream, 'should be respected. Nothing prostitutes it. It is the agent of the spirit much more than the splendid colours of the palette or the prism.'

Leunig's spectrum of imagery takes in angels, fairies and star-fields at one end, and at the other, bums, dicks, dead dogs and pubic hair. This range in itself shows his good faith: but it also allows him large freedoms, by increasing the depths of meaning he can quarry from what is apparently trivial and quotidian.

Look at his picture of the interior of a bus divided into two areas, farting and non-farting.

The farters sit with upright spines, frankly acknowledging their flawed human state and engaging in merry, carefree sociability. The non-farters, by comparison, sit hunched in identical postures of isolation, too dismal to raise their eyes from the floor, and enveloped in a dark and noxious haze of repression.

The shout of laughter that this provokes comes not merely from his simple play on smoking and non-smoking, but from a much deeper split that the cartoon touches on: a fundamental division between innocence and guilt, freedom and punishment, heaven and hell. Our laughter here is like the adrenalin rush we experience in our initial response to a poem or a piece of music 'where sweets compacted lie': it is a sudden release of the complex force that the work condenses.

UNLIKE much modern cartooning, in the *New Yorker* for example, Leunig's work often does not rely on captions. A father, chin in hand at the table, stares in gloomy awe at his child drawing, its manic, joyful, unselfconscious productiveness. A sunbaking girl wakes to find that her pubic hair has been stolen by a bird and turned into a treetop nest. An angel in flight looks down from a black, seething sky, his mouth and eyes rounded with alarm, and without being shown it we know that the cause of his horror is *our world*.

Leunig himself, at times, contemplates the world with horror. Horror, but not disgust, and never without hope. The self he senses as divided. A man berates a tiny heart in a cage:

2

'Sing, damn you — SING!' The heart remains silent. He explodes into a rage, rains blows against the bars, becomes a whirl of violence. The storm passes. The cage is bent and twisted now, but the heart inside it, though still silent, is unscathed.

Nor are Leunig's angels stone-eyed bearers of divine judgement. They are helpful, anxious creatures with tatty wings and daggy little nighties — airborne versions of our better selves. One offers a kiss through the bars to a man trapped in a sewer. Others alight eagerly to take grain from the hand of a person on a park bench. They are not immune to our savagery: the most gruesome drawing in all Leunig's work (not included here — its original has gone missing) shows an angel submitting, shocked, to the amputation of its wings by an officious fellow wielding a pair of long-handled hedge-clippers; but their aim is to bless and to comfort, and there are times when Leunig's sky is crowded with them.

Likewise, in his world of stir-crazy domesticity, crashing mutual misunderstandings, and panic in the dark air of modern cities, a man and a woman can still approach each other awkwardly, bearing gifts, out of their respective gender chasms. A child can admire his father for clowning in the dark with a ukulele. A man can devise and categorise six different styles of purgative weeping. And a serious student of life can set up, on a hill overlooking the city, a wonderful piece of scientific equipment called an UNDERSTANDASCOPE: he points it at the swarming spectacle below, he bends forward, he sends his gaze keenly through the tube — and this collection of Michael Leunig's is what he sees.

Helen Garner
March 1991

An introductory confession

ONCE UPON a time I used to be a political cartoonist. I worked for a Melbourne newspaper called *Newsday* but I had trouble making witty, incisive jokes.

One Saturday morning in 1969, struggling towards a deadline and trying to draw a cartoon about the Vietnam war, a strange thing happened to me. In an act of merry insolence; as a small rebellion against deadlines, punchlines and politics I sidestepped my obligations and the grave topic in hand and drew what I thought was an absurd, irresponsible triviality. Tempting fate, I presented it to the editor for publication.

It showed a man riding towards the sunset on a large duck. On his head he wore a teapot. Not a 'proper' cartoon by conventional standards, quite loopy in fact, but a joyous image nevertheless.

The editor told me he didn't know what it meant but laughed, shook his head and published it. I suspect that deep down, to my good fortune, he understood.

Many years later I was able to interpret the meaning of this drawing with certitude.

The man was most definitely me and the teapot, worn like a fool's cap, symbolized warmth, nourishment and domestic familiarity. The duck represented feelings of primal freedom and playfulness; qualities sadly lacking, I thought, from the world of political commentary and critical awareness.

Innocently I had drawn my impending departure from political cartooning, my flight to freedom. In a moment of perversity and release I had drawn my liberating image.

In the wake of this drawing I at once began to express my most personal self with less embarrassment; to play with my ideas more freely; to bring warmth into my work; to focus on modest, everyday situations and nature as sources of imagery and to see my work as nourishing rather than mocking or hurtful.

I experimented my way onward with feelings of mischief and fertility and as I found my feet I began to find my symbols and characters. A small, wide-eyed creature with a huge nose evolved off the end of my nib: a naked angel; wingless, ageless and genderless; an innocent messenger-fool presenting no possible threat and therefore permitted to state any case or express any feeling shamelessly.

Years passed and Mr Curly arrived on a bicycle, a large perky curl rising frond-like from his head; drawn that way because it felt right and looked funny. But the curl turned out to be the tender, unfurling motion of nature's growth; the unfolding consciousness; the way in which the heart reaches out into the world.

And sailing over the horizon in a battered armchair came Vasco Pyjama, the brave searcher who left all that was understood and safe to circumnavigate his own world.

The joy of these arrivals however was matched by the pain of sudden, unexpected departures, depressions and loss of confidence when the hand and the heart could not draw or refused to draw: errors, failures and humiliations when everything seemed to collapse into foolishness and squalor.

And in the gloom of these interminable periods friends and comrades leaned close to whisper prayers of encouragement and comfort. Others came from behind to steal and wound and confound. It's traditional. The best drawing ink is bitter and sweet and salty.

YET MY moon always hung faithfully in the sky; constant companion, luminous and remote, gentle symbol of mystery, femininity and nocturnal wisdom.

I have developed a deep affection for my abiding characters and symbols, they nourish me greatly. Many times since the duck and teapot revelation their strange antics and adventures have anticipated the course my life would take. I respect their integrity and eccentric ways to an absurd degree. They appear off the end of the pen, at that wondrous point of connection and delight, and place themselves freely in my drawings. They ask for things and do what they will. They surprise, disturb and inspire me. I observe them with bemusement and respect. I let them be and eventually I hear what they are telling me.

Michael Leunig
March 1991

Age 16 July 1988; pen and ink, wash; 16.5 x 24 cm

Age 9 May 1980; pen and ink; 10 x 20 cm
Age 17 October 1987; pen and ink; 12 x 16 cm

The Museum of Manners

Age 15 January 1983; pen and ink, wash; 17 x 25 cm

Nation Review 16 September 1972; pen and ink, wash; 11 x 15.5 cm

'Ahoy there!'

Nation Review *15 February 1974; pen and ink, wash; 18 x 24.5 cm*

Nation Review *18 August 1977; pen and ink; 15.5 x 24.5 cm*

A Field Guide to Disposable Drink Containers

The First Condoms of Spring

Age 30 May 1987; pen and ink, wash; 15 x 20 cm
Age 5 September 1987; pen and ink, wash; 17 x 21 cm

CHRISTMAS TELEPHONES

cordless car phone

teapot phone

phone with memory, redial and pop-up toaster

redial phone with zoom lens, auto focus and cordless electric screwdriver

phone with calculator, auto-teller, video game five time zones coffee brewer with graphic equalizer

Bicentennial laser phone with aloe vera, water resist to 50m. with bar coding quartz-halogen compact disc nervous breakdown with four-wheel-drive solar heated swimming pool.

HELLO

leunig

Age 26 November 1988; pen and ink; 12.5 x 16 cm

'The one on the left is a yuppy. The one on the right is a dinky. Behind them is a trendy and next to the trendy is a hippy . . . then down past the monkeys are some more dinkies looking at the donkeys.'

Age 18 July 1987; pen and ink, wash; 16 x 23 cm

Age 8 October 1988; pen and ink, wash; 14 x 19.5 cm

Age 31 December 1988; pen and ink; 17 x 22 cm

19

Mr Curly sees 'The Great Impressionists' at the National Gallery in Canberra.

Age 14 July 1984; pen and ink, wash; 16 x 23 cm

'I just feel so incredibly free!'

Age 3 December 1983; pen and ink, wash; 16 x 19 cm

Plastic Shopping Bags in Autumn

Age 25 March 1989; pen and ink, wash; 16 x 27.5 cm

Age 24 June 1989; pen and ink, wash; 18.5 x 27.5 cm

23

Age 28 May 1988; pen and ink, wash; 16 x 19 cm

Age 1 July 1986; pen and ink, wash; 12.5 x 17.5 cm
Age 10 June 1989; pen and ink; 9.5 x 22.5 cm

25

Age 9 July 1983; pen and ink, wash; 15 x 12 cm

HOW TO GET THERE

Go to the end of the path until you get to the gate.

Go through the gate and head straight out towards the horizon.

Keep going towards the horizon.

Sit down and have a rest every now and again.

But keep on going. Just keep on with it

Keep on going as far as you can. That's how you get there

Leunig

Age 26 May 1990; pen and ink; 15 x 19 cm

Age 16 June 1990; pen and ink; 20 x 15 cm

Mr Curly Comes Home

Nation Review *30 November 1973; pen and ink, wash; 20 x 23 cm*

Nation Review *30 April 1976 pen and in 10 x 13 cm*

31

'Gee Dad . . . You're fantastic!'

Nation Review *26 February 1972; pen and ink, wash; 20 x 27 cm*

Nation Review 27 June 1971; pen and ink, wash; 16 x 24 cm

33

Nation Review *12 February 1972; pen and ink, wash; 21.5 x 27 cm*

Age 12 November 1983; pen and ink, wash; 16 x 20 cm

Age 30 March 1985; pen and ink; 12 x 16.5 cm

36

Age 13 August 1983; pen and ink, wash; 17 x 21 cm
Age 22 August 1987; pen and ink, wash; 12 x 16 cm

37

Nation Review *24 June 1972; pen and ink, wash; 28 x 28 cm*

Nation Review 3–9 May 1974; pen and ink, wash; 20 x 25 cm

Age 8 December 1984; pen and ink, wash; 17 x 25 cm

Age 17 December 1983; pen and ink, wash; 14 x 22 cm

41

Age 11 June 1983; pen and ink, wash; 15 x 19 cm

42

Nation Review 1970–75; pen and ink, wash; 16 x 15 cm

Age 28 March 1988; pen and ink, wash; 18 x 26cm

44

Come sit down beside me
I said to myself.
And although it doesn't make sense
I held my own hand
As a small sign of trust
And together I sat on the fence.

Nation Review *6 April 1973; pen and ink, wash; 14 x 10 cm*

Now I lay me down to sleep
I pray thee Lord my soul to sweep
Yes sweep it with your mighty broom
Until it's like a tidy room
All neat and clean with doors shut tight
And curtains drawn against the light
The neatest, darkest piece of gloom
My soul, my locked and empty room.

Nation Review *15 August 1975; pen and ink, wash; 16 x 17 cm*

THE MIRROR.

Each year my mirror seems much older
Somewhat duller and a fraction colder
The glass which always gleamed and twinkled
Now appears all scratched and wrinkled

Appears more blotchy, tired and droopy
Confused and haggard, dazed and loopy
Sadder, slower, grimmer, glummer
I think that I've been sold a bummer.

leunig

Age 31 December 1988; pen and ink, wash; 12 x 16 cm

When the heart
Is cut or cracked or broken
Do not clutch it
Let the wound lie open

Let the wind
From the good old sea blow in
To bathe the wound with salt
And let it sting.

Let a stray dog lick it
Let a bird lean in the hole and sing
A simple song like a tiny bell
And let it ring

Leunig

Age 15 October 1988; pen and ink, wash; 12 x 16 cm

Let it go. Let it out.
Let it all unravel.
Let it free and it can be
A path on which to travel.

Age 2 December 1989; pen and ink, wash; 17.5 x 28 cm

'Waiter, there's a hair in my soup!'

Age 28 July 1988; pen and ink; 7 x 5 cm
Nation Review 1 December 1972; pen and ink, wash; 13 x 17 cm

Nation Review 23 September 1972; pen and ink; 9 x 15 cm
The Travelling Leunig, Penguin 1988; pen and ink; 6 x 6 cm

Nation Review 4 July 1975; pen and ink, wash; 18.5 x 25 cm

Nation Review 19 February 1972; pen and ink, wash; 19 x 28 cm

Nation Review *15 March 1974; pen and ink, wash; 12 x 11 cm*

Nation Review 15 October 1971; pen and ink, wash; 20.5 x 25 cm

Age 23 June 1984; pen and ink, wash; 16 x 22 cm

Nation Review *12 October 1973; pen and ink, wash; 18 x 23 cm*

Nation Review 25 March 1972; pen and ink; wash; 24 x 30 cm

Age 15 November 1982; pen and ink; 13 x 20 cm

59

One sunny day you look down and there it is at your feet... a tiny piece of gold.

You pick it up and as you do you notice the vein in a rock where it came from

Excitedly you begin to dig.... you follow the vein downwards.

Down, down.... away from the sun... you work earnestly and the years pass.

Deeper you follow the lead. Smashing at the rock face.... propping the tunnel... exhausting yourself.

You begin to fear a cave-in and by now it is too dark to see the gold.

All you can do is feel its weight in your hands.

Back on the surface is another beautiful sunny day.... the same as it ever was.

Leunig

Age 24 May 1982; pen and ink; 14 x 19.5 cm

Age 20 August 1988; pen and ink, wash; 18 x 20 cm

61

Age 21 May 1983; pen and ink, wash; 15.5 x 18 cm

Modern Australian tragedies: the collapsing pool

Age 28 December 1985; pen and ink, wash; 12 x 16 cm

Age 2 April 1988; pen and ink, wash; 16 x 12 cm

Age 4 December 1982; pen and ink; 15.5 x 21 cm

Age 30 August 1982; pen and ink; 14 x 18.5 cm

Age 28 April 1987; pen and ink, wash; 13.5 x 8.5 cm

Age 5 October 1982; pen and ink; 14 x 10 cm

Vasco Pyjama in the Strait of a Thousand Lighthouses

Nation Review *6 September 1974; pen and ink, wash; 17 x 25.5 cm*

Age 18 August 1990; pen and ink, wash; 11.5 x 16 cm

Age 26 March 1988; pen and ink, wash; 15 x 19 cm

71

Age 14 July 1990; pen and ink, wash; 12 x 15.5 cm

Age 18 May 1985; pen and ink, wash; 16 x 12 cm

73

Age 9 April 1983; pen and ink, wash; 15 x 21 cm

74

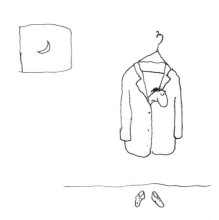

Nation Review *18 October 1974; pen and ink; 8 x 9 cm*   Nation Review *19 March 1976; pen and ink; 10 x 7 cm*
Nation Review *1970–75; pen and ink; 10 x 8 cm*   Nation Review *16 January 1976; pen and ink; 6 x 6 cm*

Age 17 March 1984; pen and ink, wash; 15 x 18.5 cm

Age 23 April 1983; pen and ink, wash; 18 x 18 cm

'Oh give me a home where the buffalo roam, where the deer and the antelope play.'

Age 4 September 1982; pen and ink, wash; 18 x 27 cm

Nation Review 7 October 1972; pen and ink, wash; 21 x 16 cm

Nation Review 21 December 1973; pen and ink, wash; 18 x 24 cm

T-shirt 1988; pen and ink; 11.5 x 13.5 cm

Nation Review *15 September 1977; pen and ink, wash; 13.5 x 12.5 cm*
Nation Review *18 May 1973; pen and ink, wash; 15 x 17 cm*

Age 20 August 1983; pen and ink, wash; 14 x 18 cm
Age 28 July 1990; pen and ink, wash; 14 x 18 cm

CAPTION (ITALIC)

The acoustics could be better? what do you mean "the acoustics could be better"? What the hell are you talking about?

Age 13 November 1982, pen and ink, wash 19 x 24.5 cm

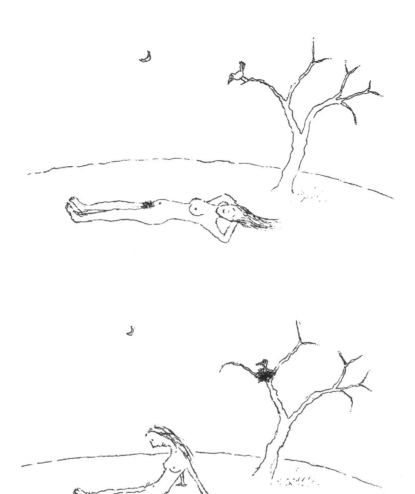

Nation Review 6 June 1975; pen and ink; 18 x 12 cm

WHY Dogs sniff each others tails.... an old but true story.

Once upon a time, when dogs ruled the earth, a gala dog ball was organised and all the dogs in the world were invited..

When the dogs arrived at the ball they checked their tails in at the cloak room as was the custom in those happy, far off days....

It was a wonderful, glittering occasion and all the dogs, regardless of breed or background, danced the night away and were thoroughly enjoying themselves until suddenly......

.... the fire alarm sounded. The ballroom was alight and an uproarious panic broke out...

The vast yelping pack stampeded to the cloak room and in the confusion the tails were mixed up.

To this day you will see them sniffing each others tails as they go about their forlorn search for their proper tails. This is the eternal aftermath of the night that THE DOG BALL CAUGHT FIRE...!

Leunig

Nation Review *27 January 1977; pen and ink; 17 x 25 cm*

Awful aspects of spring. The new dog digs up the old dog.

Age 15 September 1984; pen and ink, wash; 16 x 17.5 cm

Nation Review 1970–75; pen and ink, wash; 6 x 11 cm

The Kiss

Age 7 September 1985; pen and ink, wash; 16 x 12 cm

Nation Review 26 September 1975; pen and ink, wash; 11 x 13 cm

Nation Review 5 September 1975; pen and ink, wash; 13 x 18 cm

The harvest. The bumper crop. The Autumn Festival of Lust and Passion.

Age 12 March 1988; pen and ink, wash; 15.5 x 20.5 cm

Age 2 March 1985; pen and ink, wash; 16.5 x 23.5 cm

Age 19 July 1986; pen and ink, wash; 16 x 19 cm

'Stop admiring yourself!'

Age 18 June 1983; pen and ink, wash; 17.5 x 23 cm

95

Men and Women, War and Peace

Age 2 September 1989; pen and ink, wash; 16 x 32 cm

Age 7 October 1989; pen and ink, wash; 16 x 27 cm

97

Nation Review 30 March 1973; pen and ink, wash; 12 x 7 cm

Age 7 April 1990; pen and ink; 14.5 x 19.5 cm

Age 9 April 1989; pen and ink, wash; 12 x 16 cm

Nation Review *9 June 1977; pen and ink, wash; 13.5 x 17.5 cm*

Nation Review *26 November 1976; pen and ink, wash; 13.5 x 18 cm*

Nation Review 2 April 1976; pen and ink, wash; 17.5 x 24 cm

Nation Review *12 August 1972; pen and ink, wash; 23 x 18 cm*

Nation Review *4 March 1972; pen and ink; 31 x 23 cm*

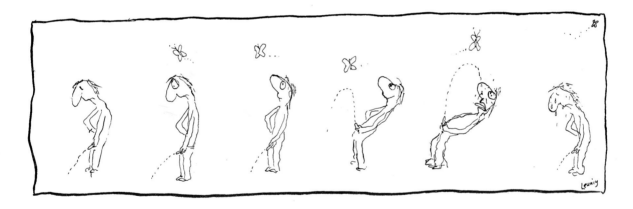

Nation Review *13 November 1971; pen and ink, wash; 11 x 13 cm*
Nation Review *3 November 1977; pen and ink; 5.5 x 18 cm*

Driving his trusty curly-mobile and accompanied by his direction-finding duck, Mr Curly takes the dangerous, winding road back to his childhood on an important mission. In the darkness he negotiates the flimsy bridge over the Great Gap. In front of him, in the glow of the headlights, Mr Curly sees wondrous shapes emerging from the gloom. Somewhere in the blackness a bell tolls. He has arrived!

Age 30 June 1990; pen and ink, wash; 17.5 x 23.5 cm

The rare phenomenon of nude fog sucking . . . note thinness of fog around sucking nude.

Nation Review 21 June 1974; pen and ink, wash; 17 x 21.5 cm

Nation Review *8 July 1972; pen and ink, wash; 24 x 33 cm*

'We're sorry to see you go Dad but we wish you well in your new life.'

Age 2 March 1988; Acrylic; 35 x 25.5 cm

Book cover, The Second Leunig: A dusty little swag, *Penguin 1979; pen and ink, wash; 15.5 x 21.5 cm*
Book cover, The Travelling Leunig, *Penguin 1990; pen and ink, wash; 11.5 x 16.5 cm*

Ramming the Shears

Book cover, Penguin 1985; pen and coloured ink on paper; 15 x 23 cm

The Sunday Drive

1990; Oil on board; 15 x 20.5 cm

The First Fleet

Age 1 January 1988; Acrylic on particle board; 69.5 x 60.5 cm

115

First Offence

1990; Plaster and oil paint on cardboard; 50 x 60 cm

116

Boy on a Bike

1989; Oil on board; 75 x 59 cm

117

Acrylic on paper; 28 x 43 cm

118

Blue Boy

1989; Oil and acrylic on cardboard; 50 x 60 cm

The Grand Final

Age 2 September 1982; Acrylic on paper; 22.5 x 43 cm